It is my belief, from
pictures come passion;
from passion comes love;
from love comes hope; and
from hope comes renewal.
In 2001, God gave "passion"
to my photography in the
form of Geri and John
Sebastian Cusenza.

In the Between... is the
response to a generous
promise the Cusenza's
made to me that day to
give unselfishly from their
Family Foundation—their
money, time, and talents.
The revenues from *In the
Between* will be used
entirely to bring education
and training to the poor
women and children in
Tanzania, East Africa.

It is important for me to
share with you my story,
as well as my work. Not
for the purpose of personal
recognition, but rather for
the encouragement of
spiritual inner-awareness.
I am living proof, that
through the love of God
there are no challenges
that can't be overcome,
if not by one, then by many.

May God bathe you in
His blessings.

Sister Rose Marie Tulacz, S.N.D.

For my family–
especially my parents.

Their love, deep faith, support,
and encouragement have been my greatest gift.

I dedicate this book to you,
Mom and Dad,
and thank you with all my heart.

forward

Before we can give our heart,

we must first possess it.

And so God lures us

In the Between

to reclaim our hearts,

only to entrust them to the world.

PHOTOGRAPHY & TEXT BY
Sister Rose Marie Tulacz, S.N.D.

Being

Life

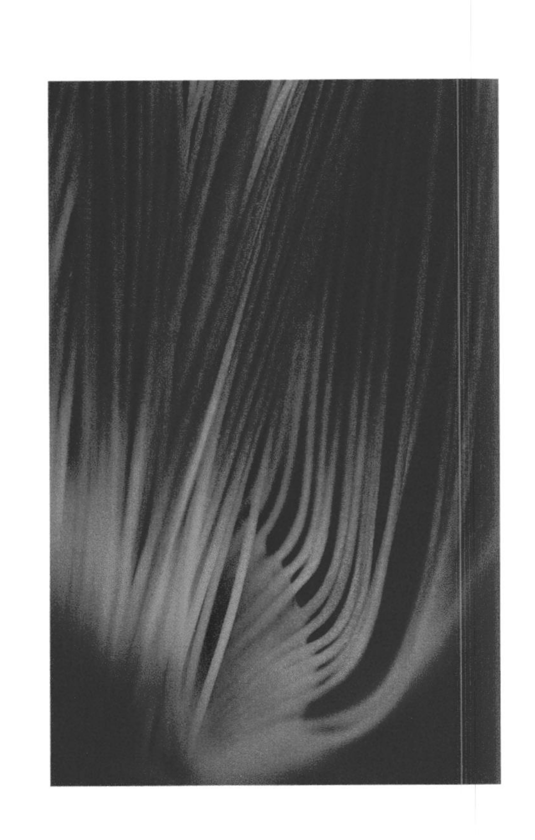

Celebration

contents

Acceptance

Everyone needs
a home!
Sister Rose Marie, [illegible]

Being

Pause and linger.

Pure color vibrations.

Journey in.

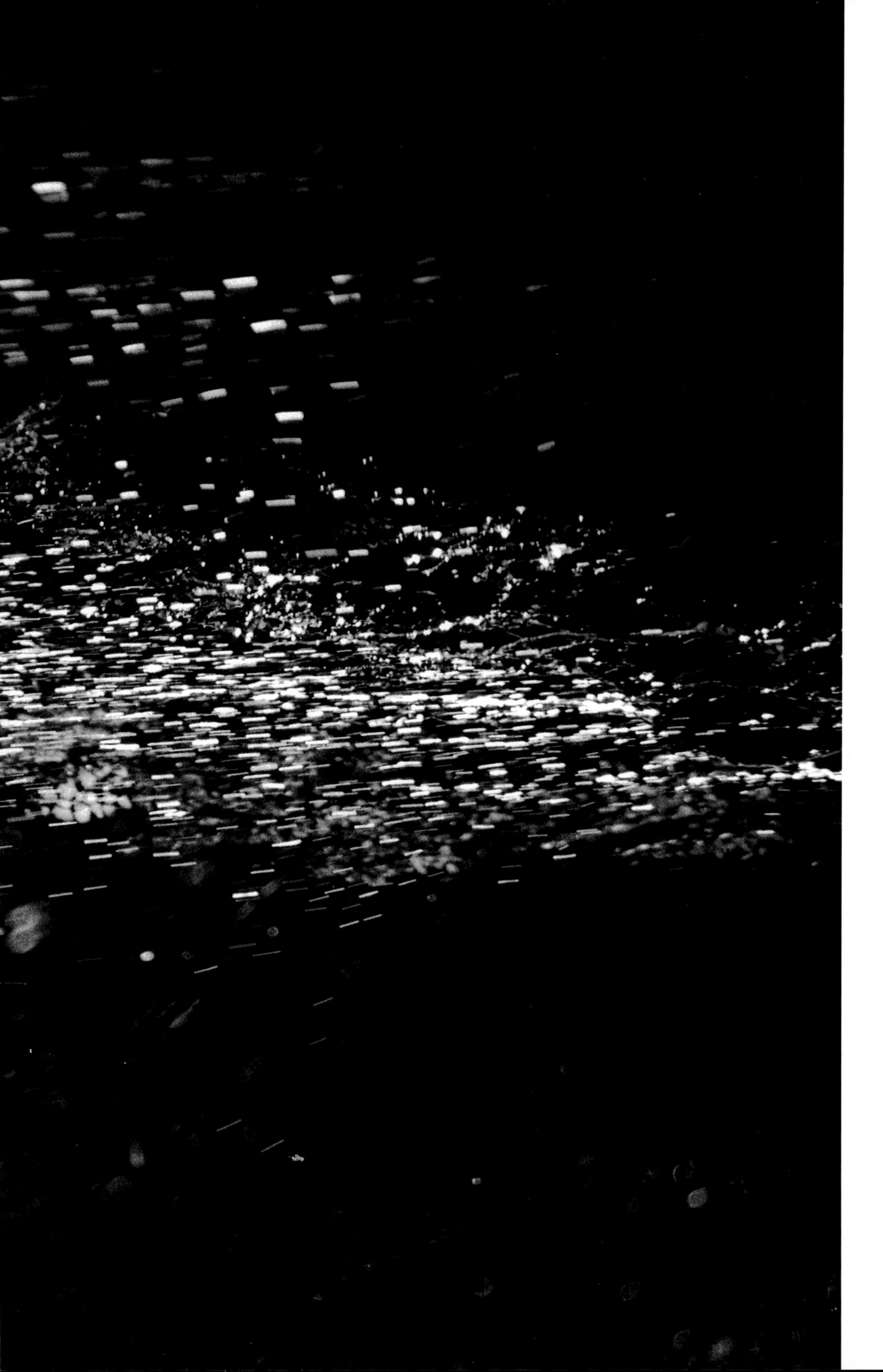

Dance
the
dance
that
beckons.

This moment, real and sacred.

Amazing beauties.

Become one

with the movement

of a sparkling pageant of wedded color

Reach in,

touch me.

My heart, my soul,

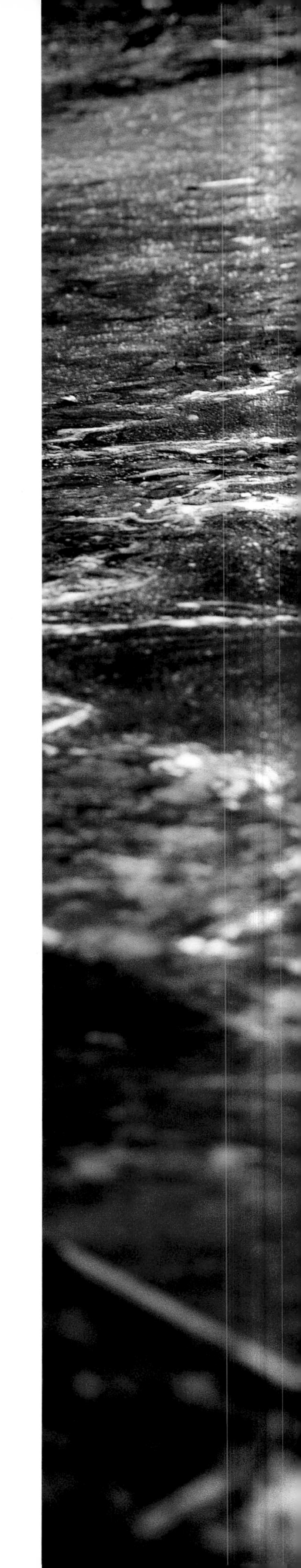

touched
by You,
the
fingertip
of God.

He whose
touch is beyond
touch has broken
through my
darkness.
I am transformed
by the earth,
by the colors
of spring.

Let me remember
that in every
vibration of color,
in each awakening
blossom,

You are there,
once again,
to touch me
with Your
loving presence.

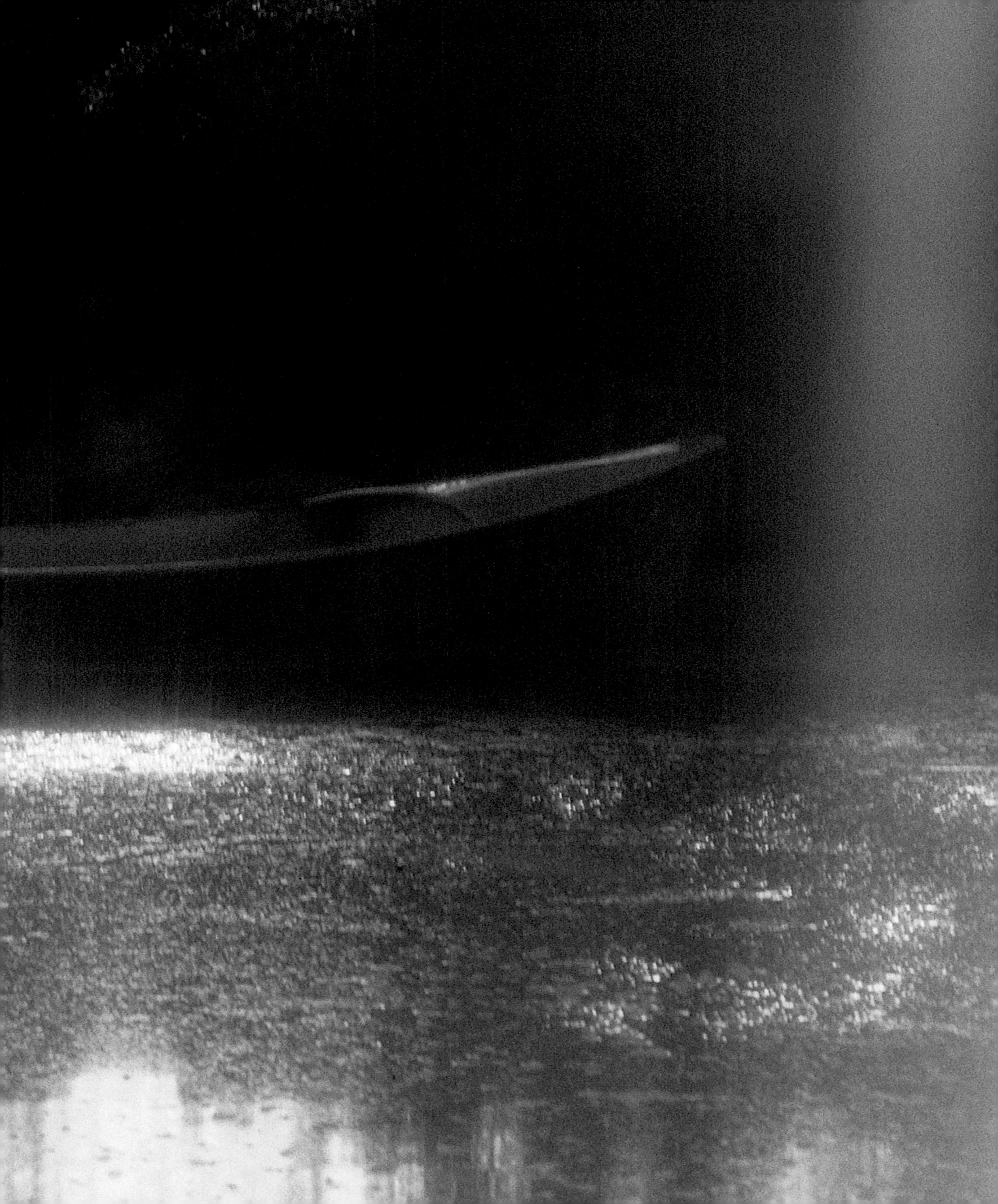

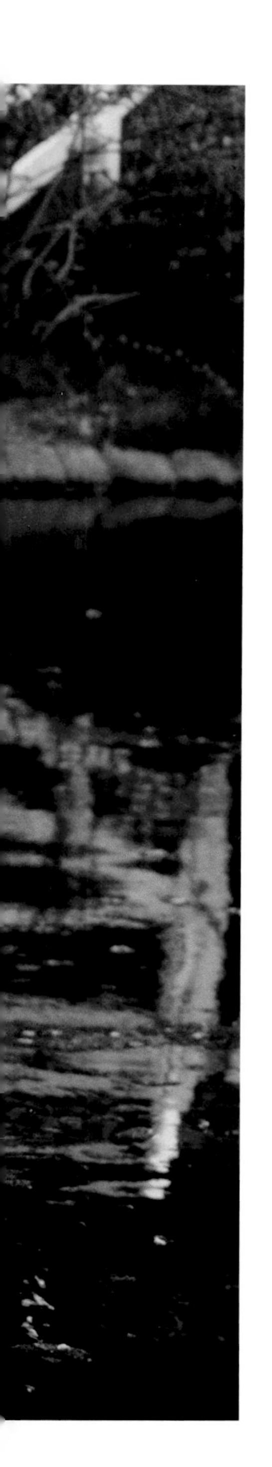

Allow life's channels of light to penetrate your soul,

enlighten your thoughts,

and bathe your existence in the joy of being one with Him.

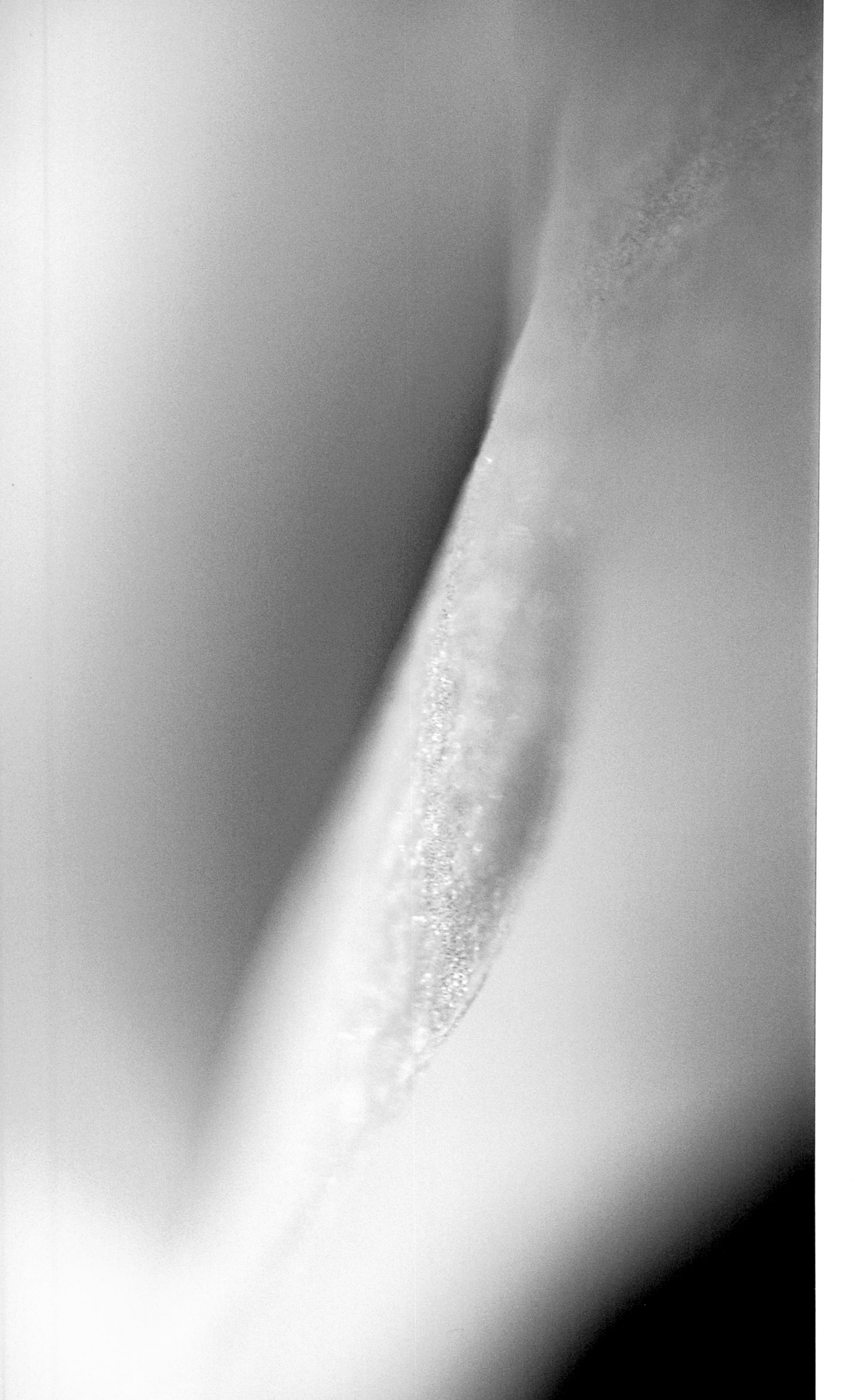

Whispers
of beauty,

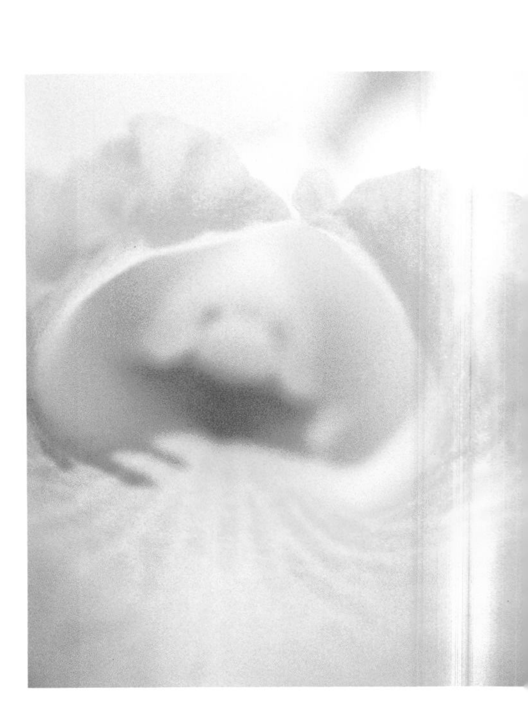

breaths of softness,

thoughts
of tranquility

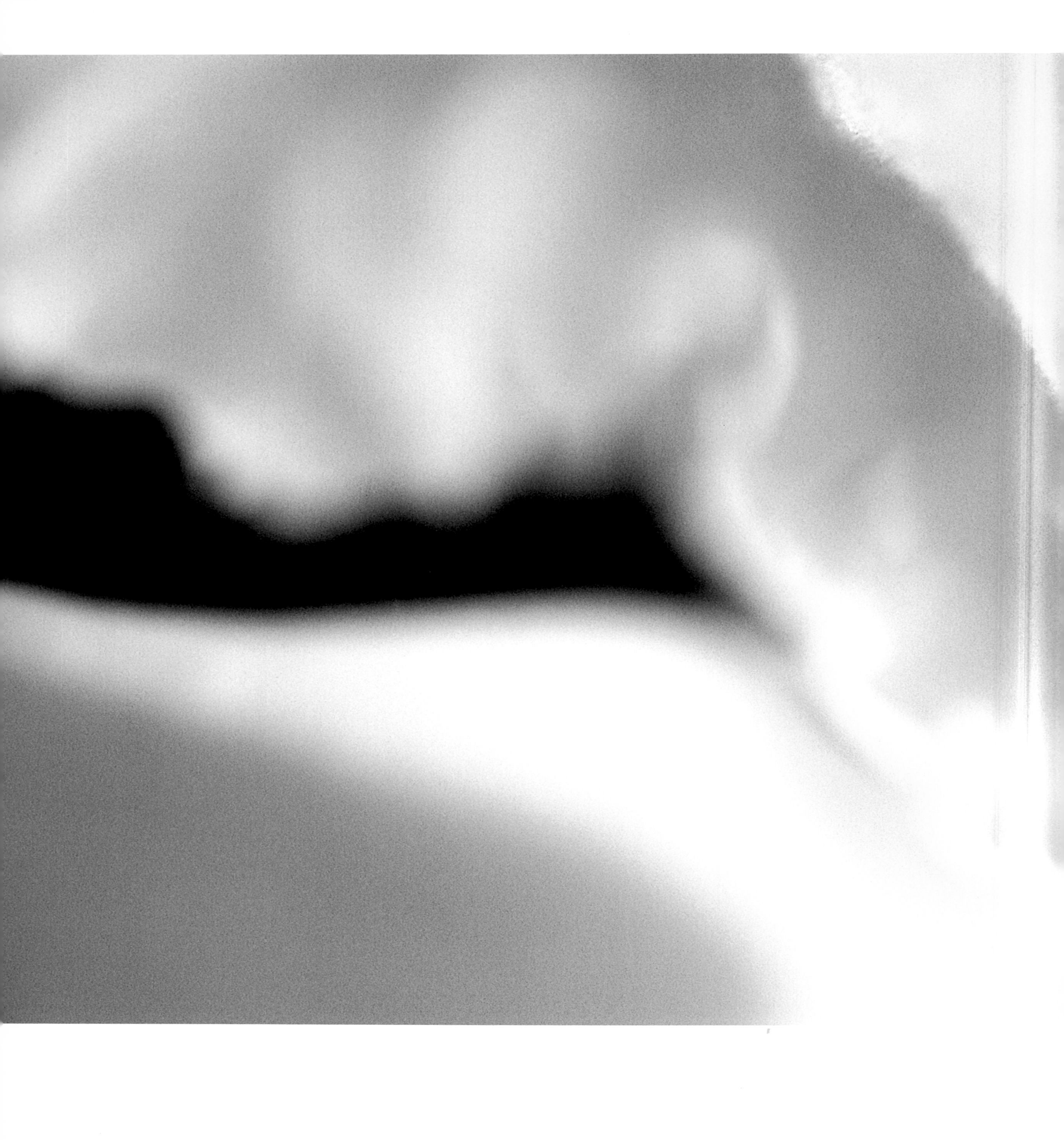

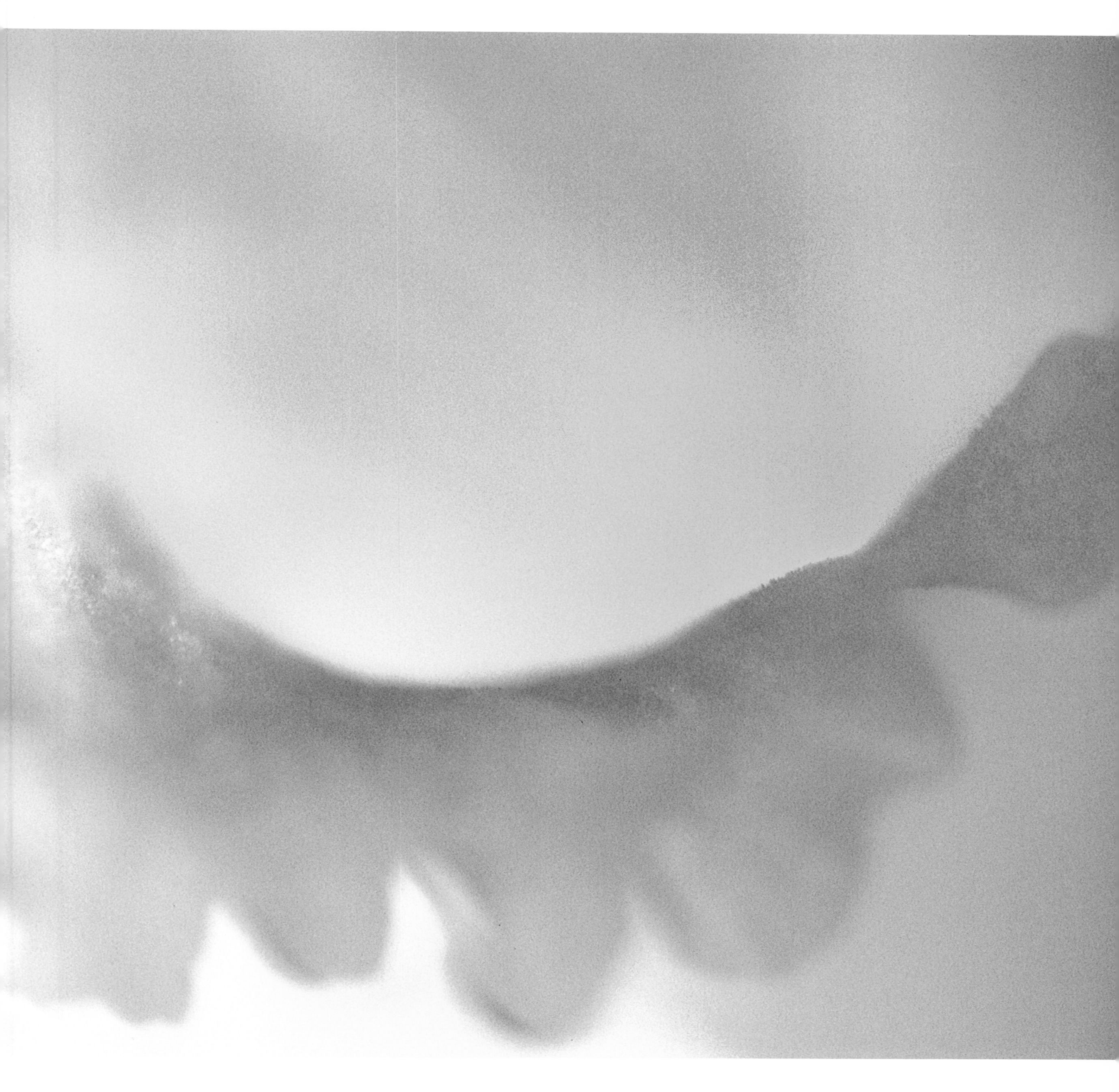

awaken my compassions,

renew
my
courage,

inflame my soul,

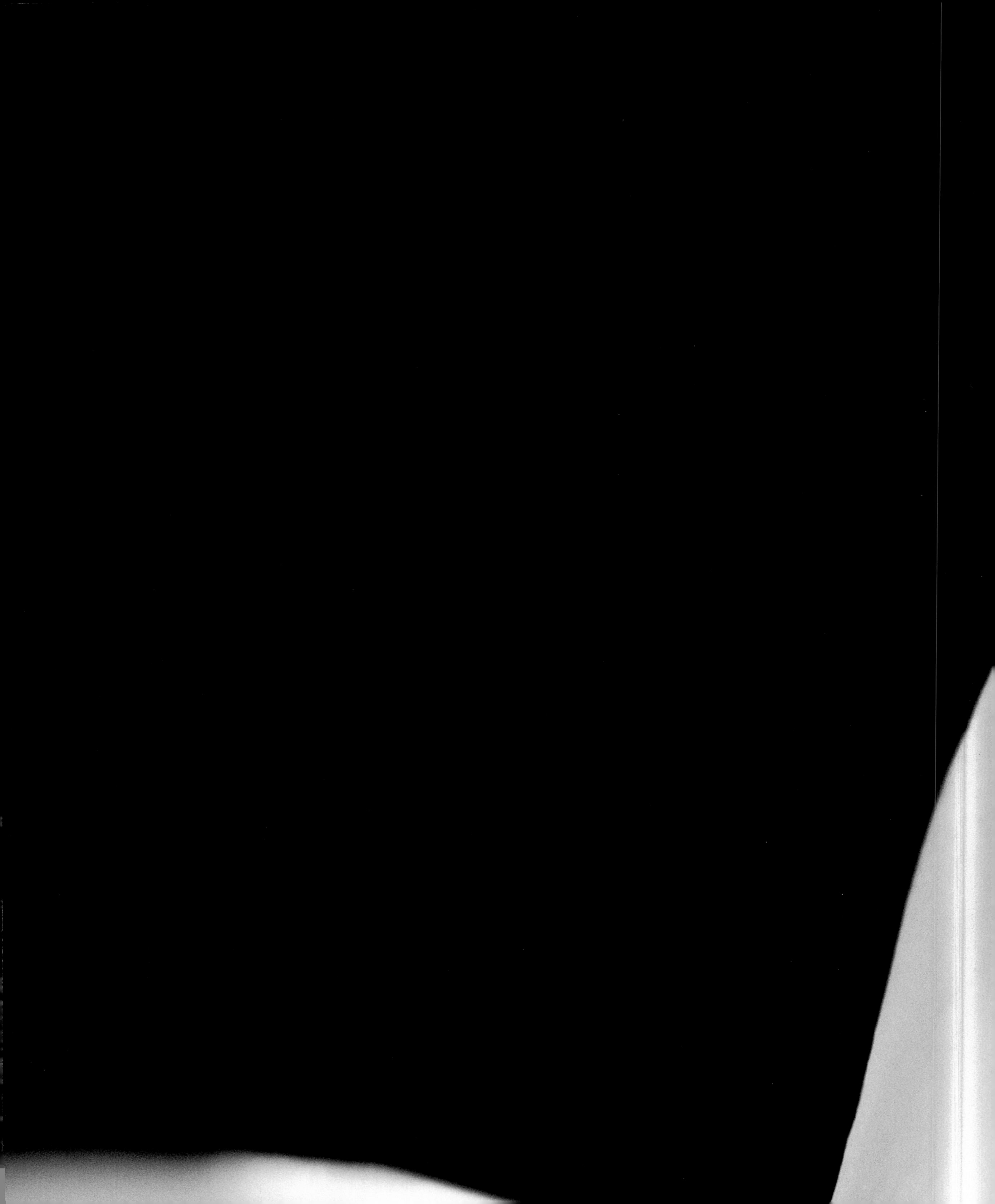

complete my fullness.

Life

I am

I am

...your seed,

...your roots,

...your vine,

I am

the thread that wraps your soul.

In darkness,
I am your sunlight.

In restlessness,
I am your peace.

In need,
I am your fulfillment.

In wealth,
I am your treasure.

Your enrichment
is My happiness,

Your growth
is My joy.

I am

as you are, the
essence of My love.

Seeds of Desire

This sunflower before me, within me. Growing in hard, unpromising soil, her seed enduring the most of what life has offered her.

Tall, with leaves outstretched—like arms calling “dance with me!” Locked into the powerful embrace of the sun. Her life is full, pure, graced under the movement of the sun. She has allowed the spell of the newborn morning to hold her gaze.

I capture the beauty of her soul as it is transformed into thousands of seeds. It is amazing how this golden canopy becomes weighed down by her abundance, yet she is not burdened by pride and excess! I marvel at her slow, steady process as she freely surrenders the fruits of her fulfillment as the light penetrates her being, my being.

The earth is desperately waiting for these precious seeds to fall and scatter. Let these seeds come over the vast fields of humanity and awaken new and unlimited fulfillment in flower and leaf!

In the past I always asked for more and more. And You have given me more. Changed am I— as light, Your light enters my soul. You are all I desire.

Like the sunflower, I bow in gratitude for this great awakening that You are enough.

Although
I
have
not
traveled
to see
the
stained
glass
windows
in the
cathedrals
of the
world...

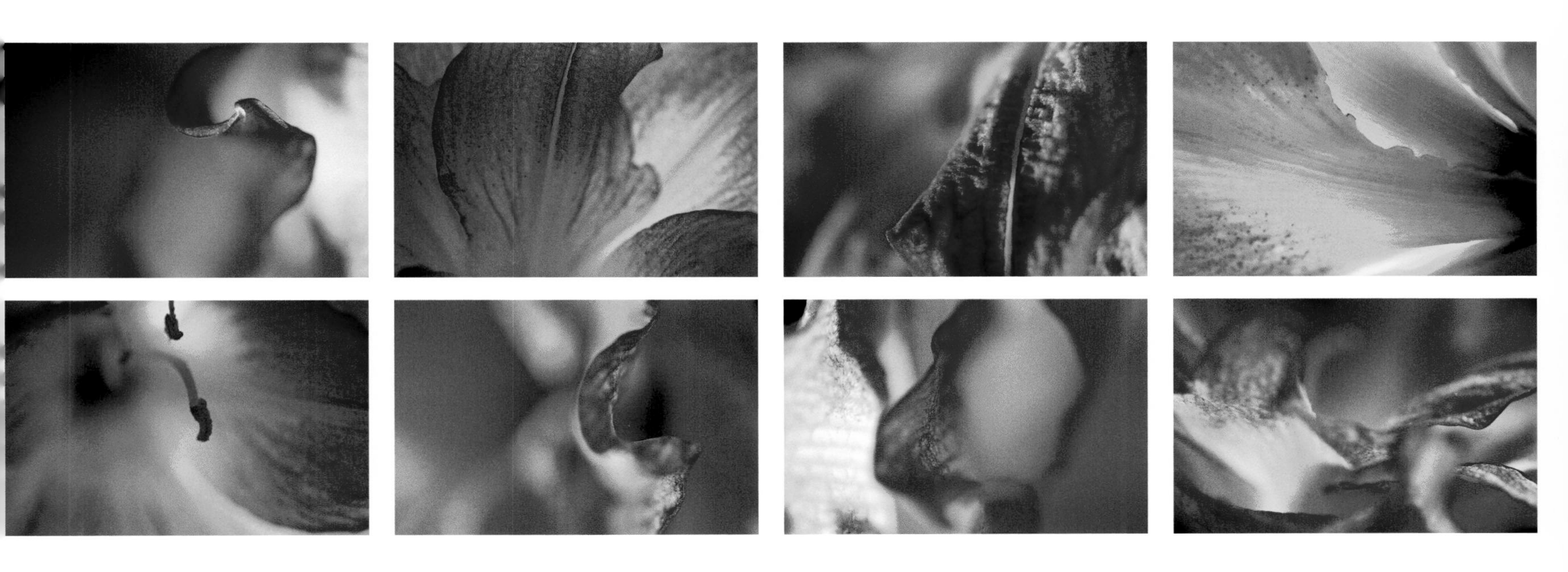

nature herself transmitts the beauty
of living light to reveal ever-changing
color, line, and form.

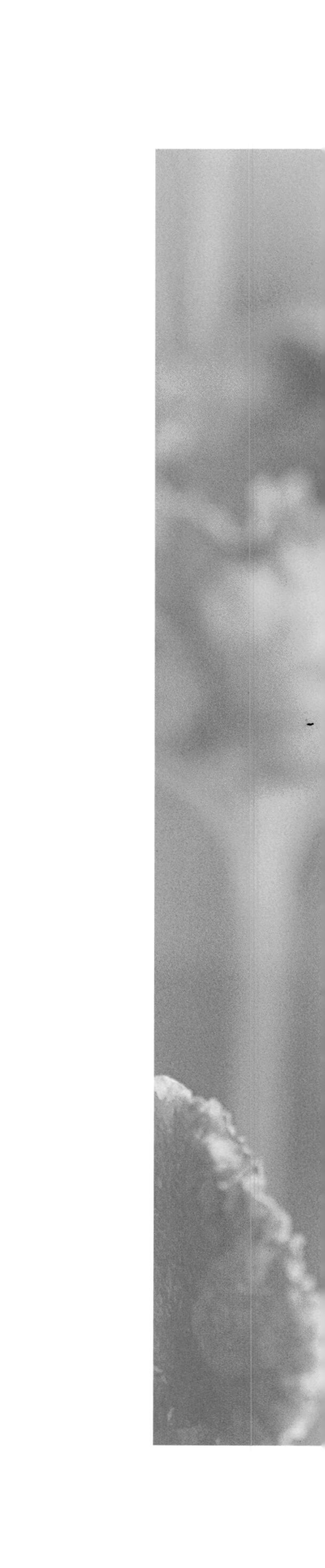

Simplicity and truth dispose the soul to be transparent, allowing the light of God's love to shine through.

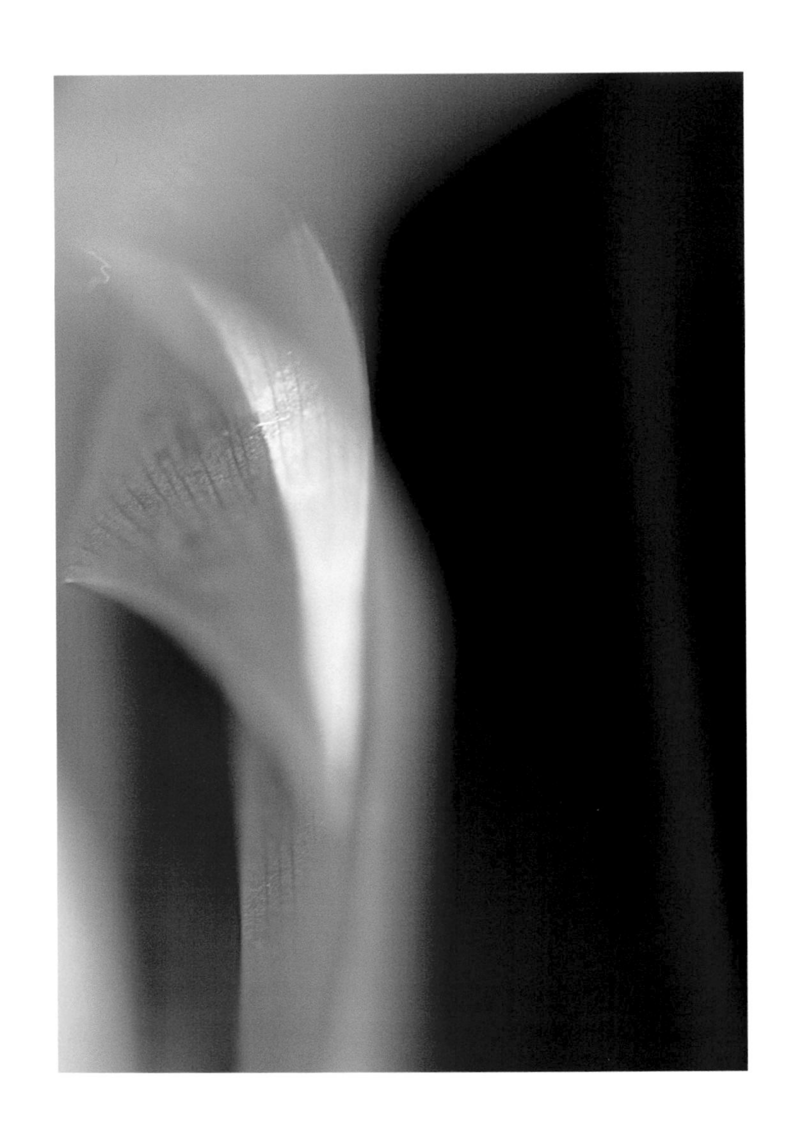

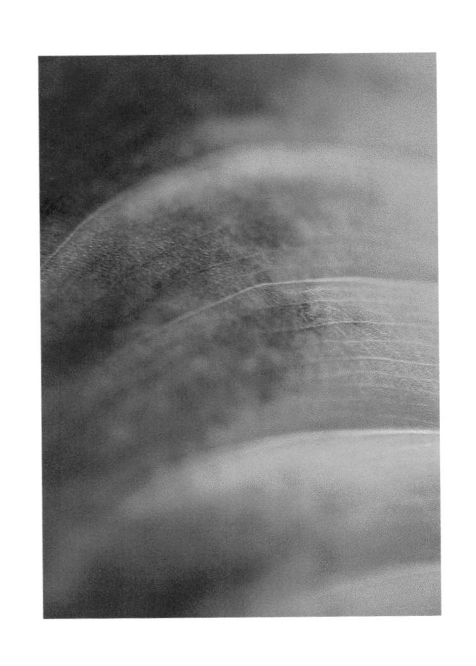

The flame of freedom burns deeply within us all. Self-liberation is nurtured in the forgiveness of others. The essence of now is ours, and ours alone. Embrace it, nurture it, live it, live by it. Be silent. Be aware. Be still. Awaken your senses to the fragrance that engulfs you. Allow this glory to manifest within you.

Accepting the past brings peace.

Living the present deepens inner purpose.

Consciousness reveals vibrant colors in celebration of this life energy.

For as within, so without.

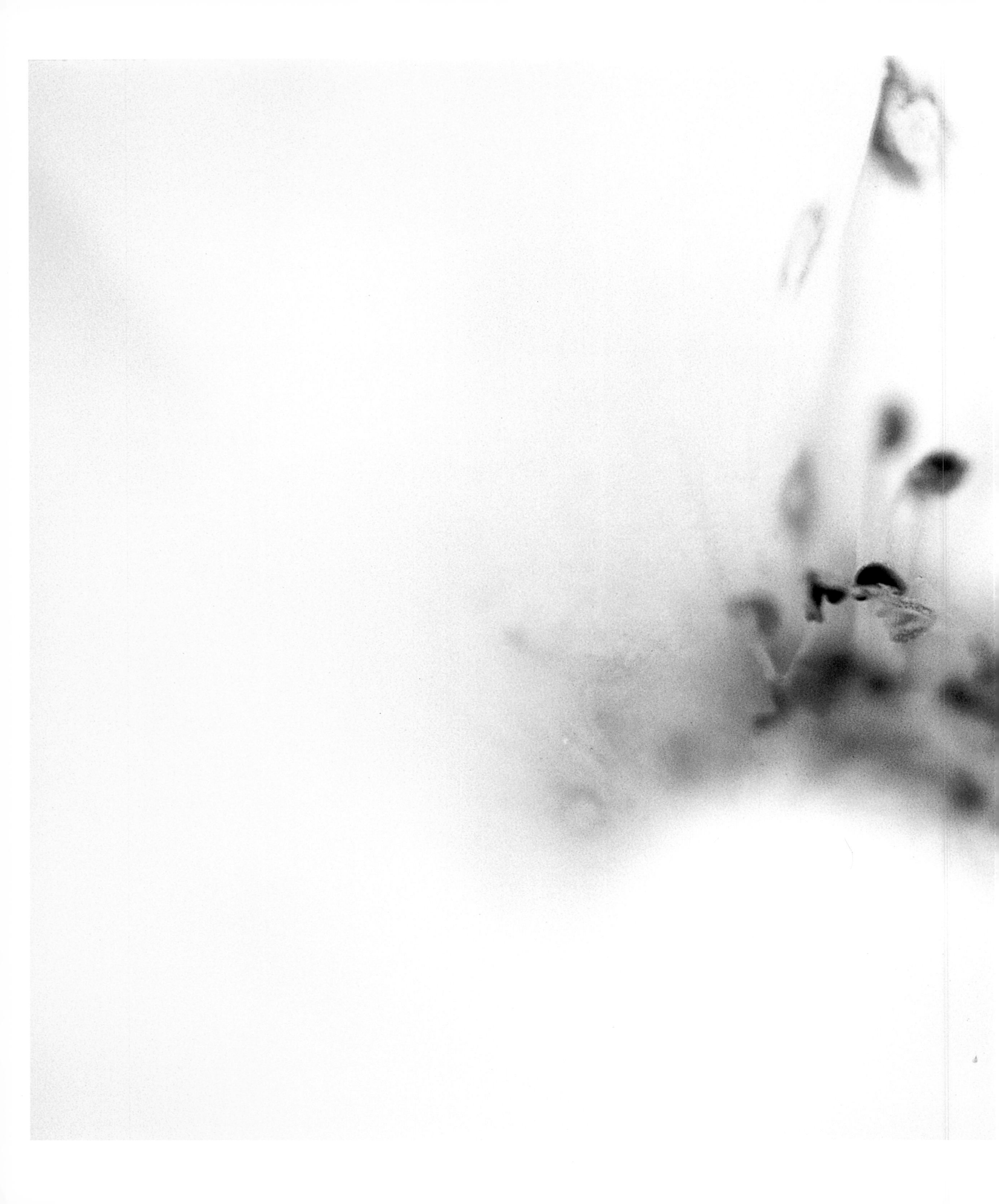

Throughout creation there are no imperfections, only uniqueness and beauty. Through struggle and triumph comes growth, from growth comes life. For the individual paths we follow bring victory and hope for all. The brilliance of God is celebrating in all shapes and colors.

Seek love

Be love

Be light and joyful,

opening and exposing the external forms of beauty, nature, and all humanity.

Sculptured images

Celebration

encapsulate light and sun

until they erupt in brilliance.

Color streams inspire, influence, empower.

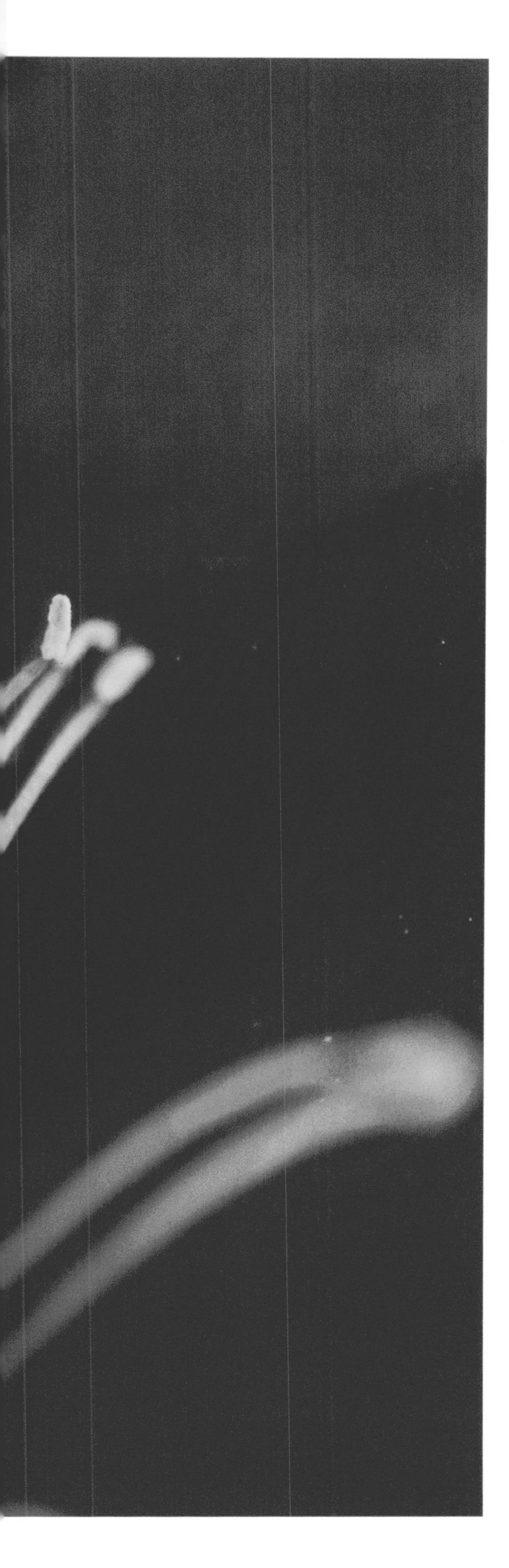

Radiating life between the known

and unknown,

awakening the flame within.

Acceptance

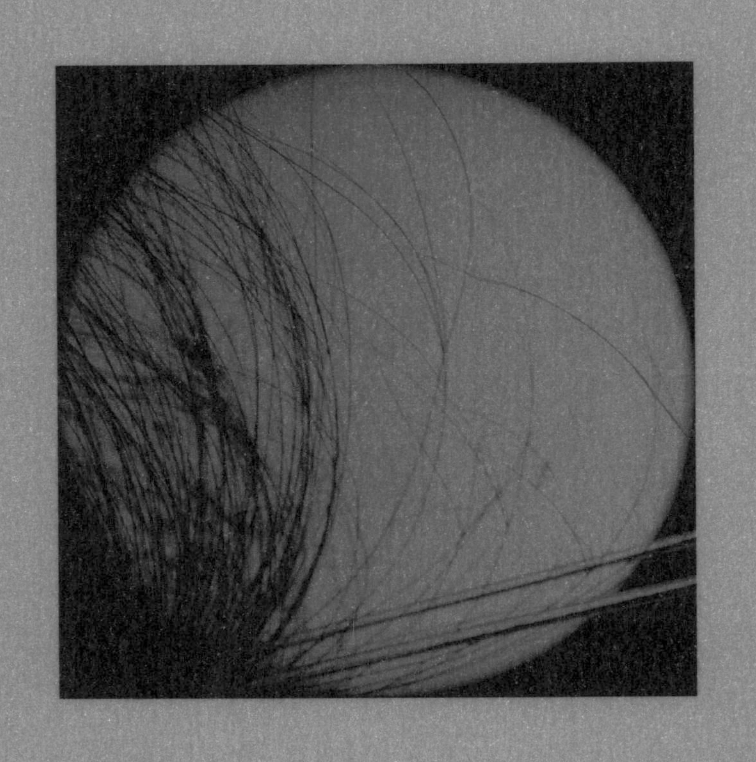

God's
mystery
beckons
in the
morning mist.
Life's jewels abound!
Light
and object
have
become
one.

A union of beauty

between

naive and innocence

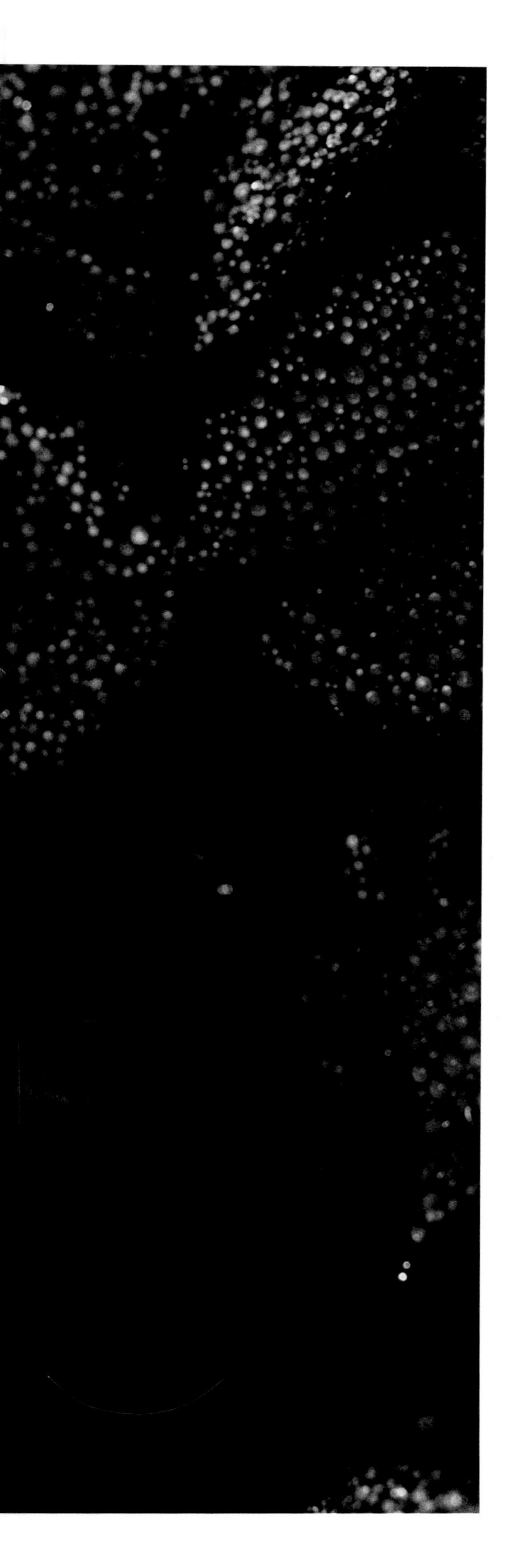

between
heaven and earth

between

dreams and reality

between

known and unknown

between

macabre and devotion

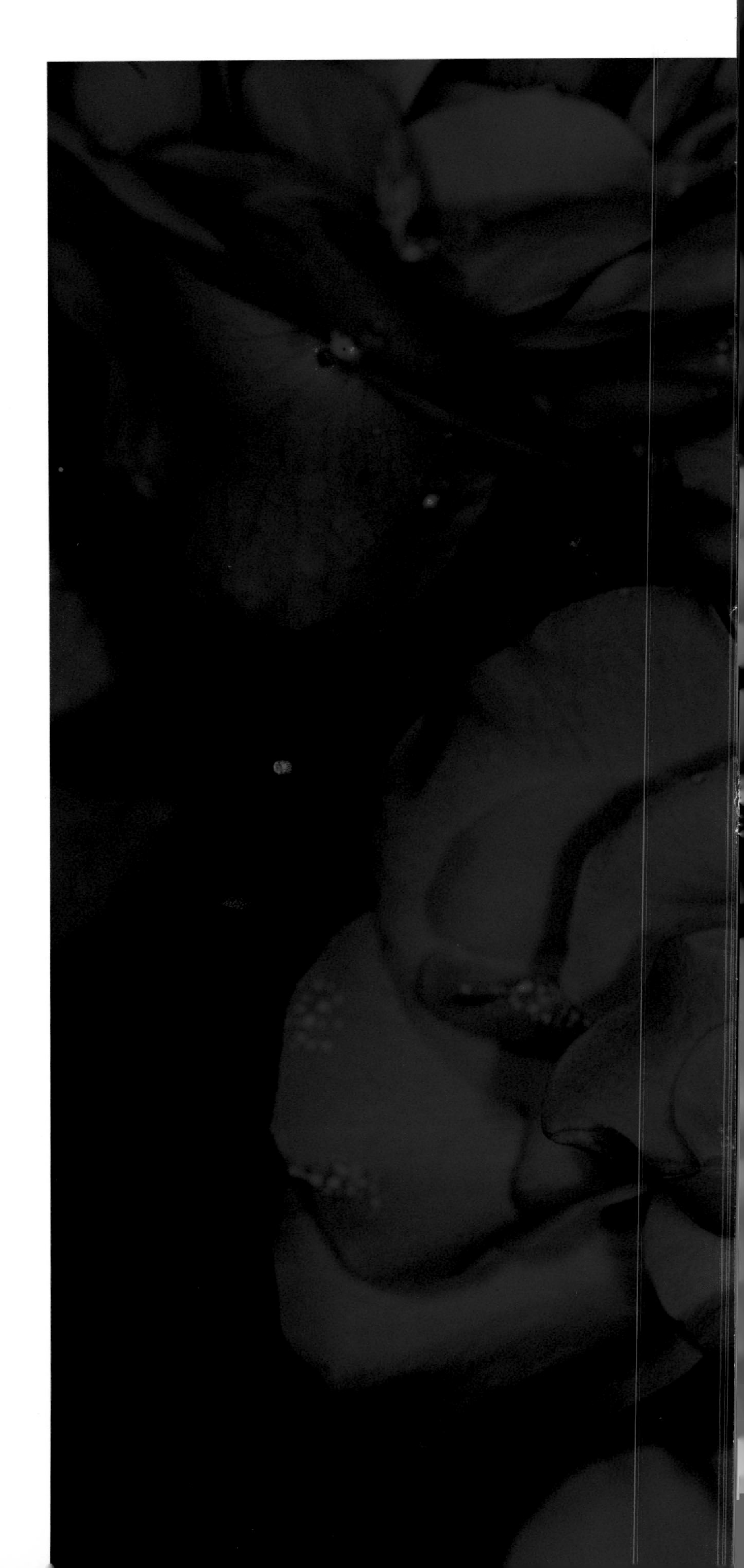

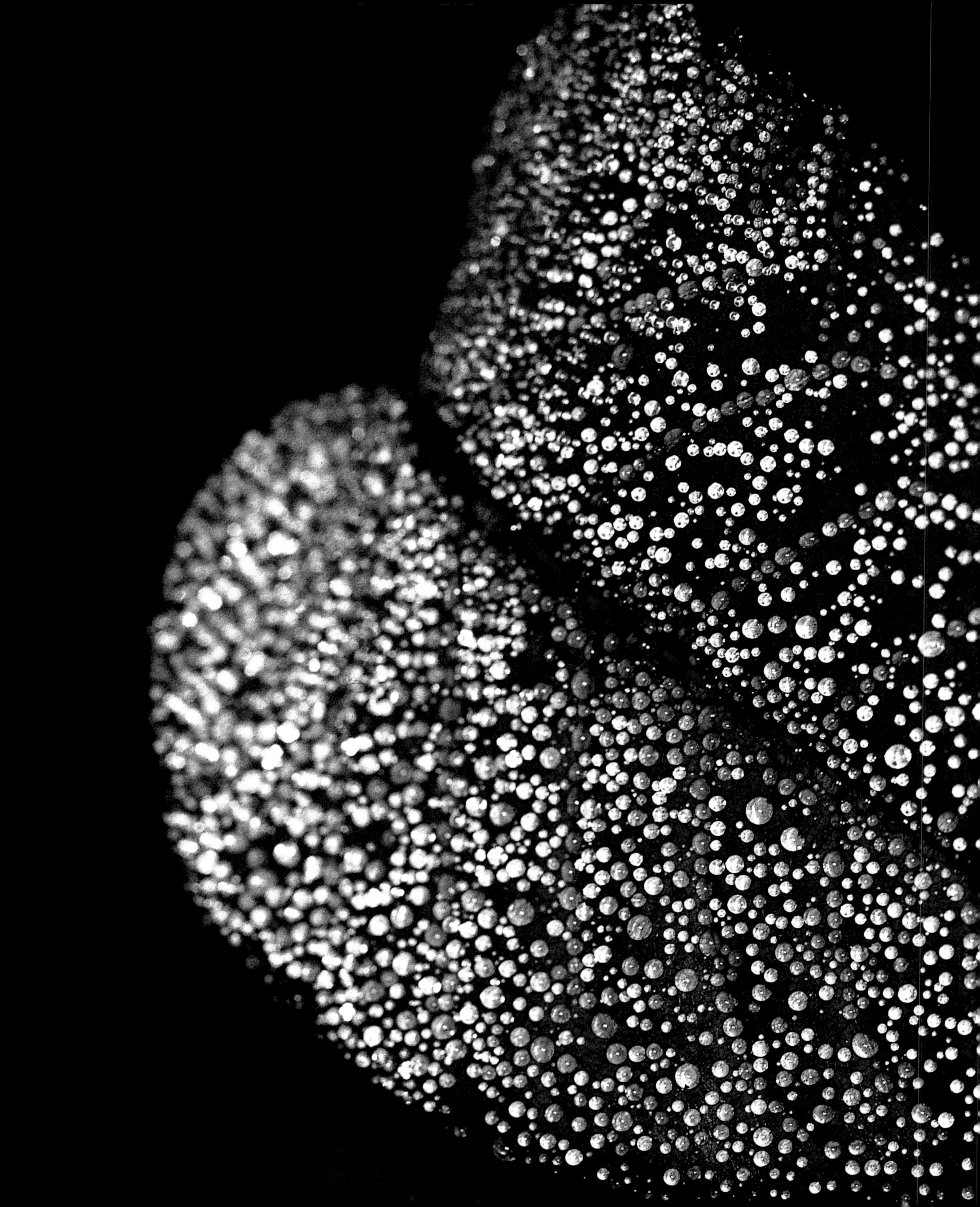

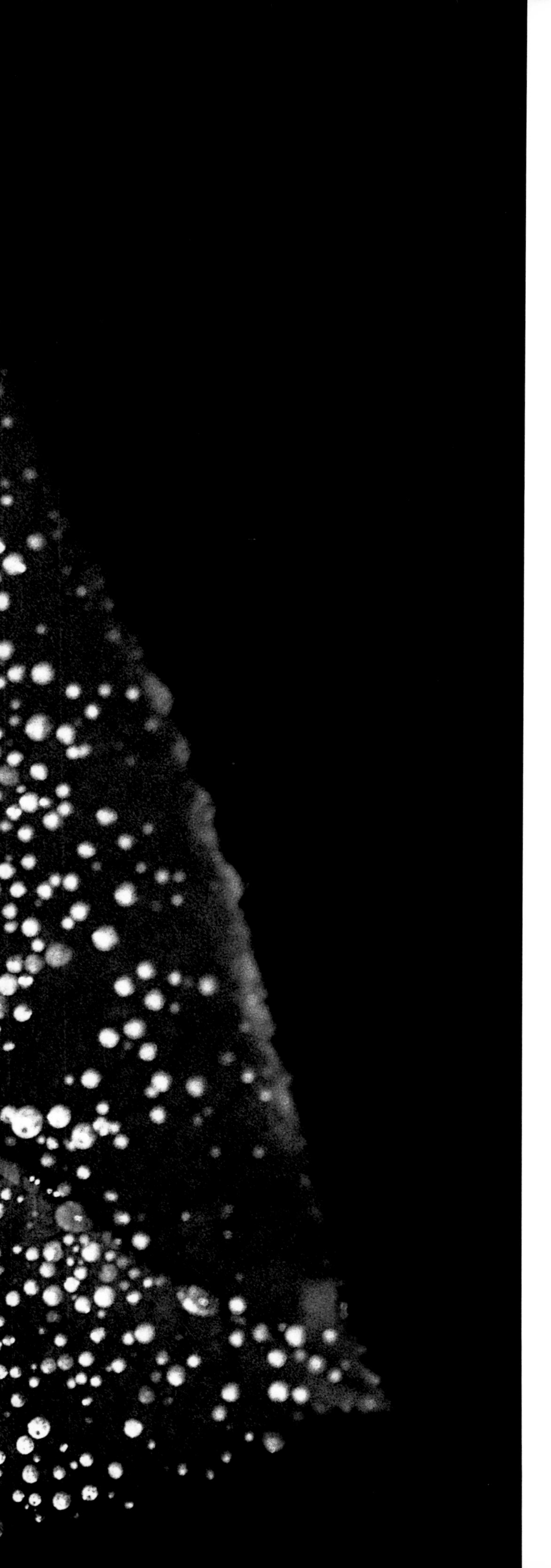

between

icon and idol.

Claim your oneness

your connectedness.

Value love in every form of

life as an expression of the

One whose life and love

is beyond all form.

Look closely.

Between

the known and the unknown.

The morning prisms hang like slivers of broken glass,
reflecting the hope of a morning song,
the notes hang like tears,
chanting words of others fears.

Somewhere

in the between,

one drop takes leave of the others,

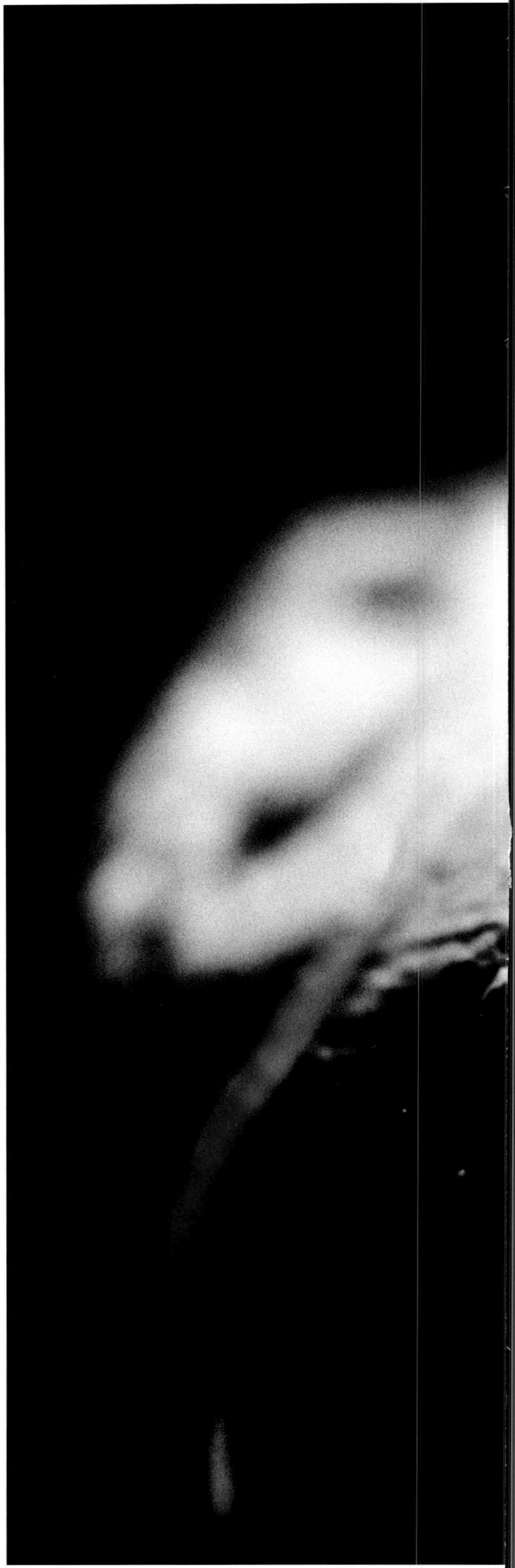

sliding down to the edge, letting go.

Falling into its true self.

Suspended.

in the between

Acceptance and surrender

are portals for the unconditional

love of God to enter.

All that is beautiful and radiant

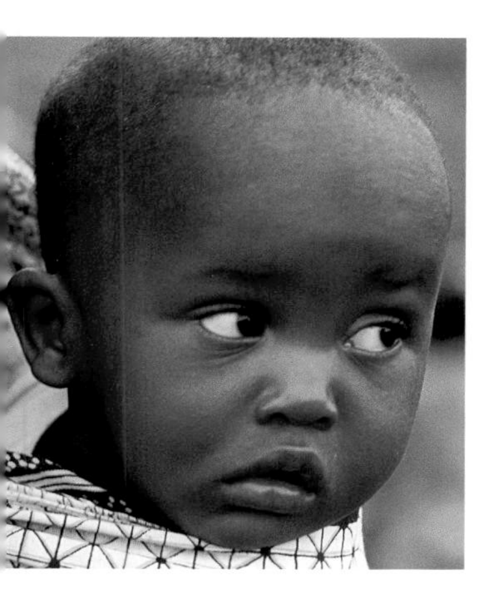

has a pre-ordained place

in His world, which belongs

first and foremost

to the poor and humbled.

poems

Pause and linger.

Pure color vibrations.

Journey in.

Light and color rises through mist of the morning dawn. Dance the dance that beckons.

This moment, real and sacred.

Amazing beauty.

Become one with the movement of a sparkling pageant of wedded color.

Reach in, touch me.

My heart, my soul, touched by You, the fingertip of God.

He whose touch is beyond touch has broken through my darkness. I am transformed by the earth, by the colors of spring. Let me remember that in every vibration of color, in each awakening blossom, You are there, once again, to touch me with Your loving presence.

Be not blinded by the clouds of ego-centrism.
Allow life's channels of light to penetrate your soul,
enlighten your thoughts,
and bathe your existence in the joy
of being one with Him.

Whispers of beauty,
Breaths of softness,
Thoughts of tranquility
Awaken my compassions,
Renew my courage,
Inflame my soul,
Complete my fullness.

I am
...your seed.
...your roots.
...your vine.
I am the thread that wraps your soul.

In darkness,
I am your sunlight.

In restlessness,
I am your peace.

In need,
I am your fulfillment.

In wealth,
I am your treasure.

Your enrichment is My happiness.
Your growth is My joy.

I am
as you are
the essence of My love.

Seeds of Desire

This sunflower before me, within me. Growing in hard, unpromising soil, her seed enduring the most of what life has offered her.

Tall, with leaves outstretched—like arms calling "dance with me!" Locked into the powerful embrace of the sun. Her life is full, pure, graced under the movement of the sun. She has allowed the spell of the newborn morning to hold her gaze.

I capture the beauty of her soul as it is transformed into thousands of seeds. It is amazing how this golden canopy becomes weighed down by her abundance, yet she is not burdened by pride and excess! I marvel at her slow, steady process as she freely surrenders the fruits of her fulfillment as the light penetrates her being, my being.

The earth is desperately waiting for these precious seeds to fall and scatter. Let these seeds come over the vast fields of humanity and awaken new and unlimited fulfillment in flower and leaf!

In the past I always asked for more and more. And You have given me more. Changed am I—as light, Your light enters my soul. You are all I desire.

Like the sunflower, I bow in gratitude for this great awakening that You are enough.

Although I have not traveled to see the stained glass windows
in the cathedrals of the world...
nature herself transmitts the beauty of living light
to reveal ever–changing color, line, and form.

Simplicity and truth
dispose the soul to be transparent,
allowing the light of God's love
to shine through.

The flame of freedom burns deeply within us all.
Self-liberation is nurtured in the forgiveness of others.

The essence of now is ours, and ours alone.
Embrace it, nurture it, live it, live by it.

Be silent. Be aware. Be still.
Awaken your senses to the fragrance that engulfs you.

Allow His glory to manifest within you.

Accepting the past brings peace.
Living the present deepens inner purpose.

Consciousness reveals vibrant colors in celebration of this life energy.
For as within, so without.

Throughout creation there are no imperfections,
only uniqueness and beauty.

Through struggle and triumph comes growth,
and from growth comes life.

For the individual paths we follow
bring victory and hope for all.

The brilliance of God is celebrated
in all shapes and colors.

Seek love. Be love.
Be light and joyful,
opening and exposing
the external forms of beauty, nature, and all humanity.

Sculptured images
encapsulate light and sun
until they erupt in brilliance.

Color streams
inspire, influence, empower.

Radiating life
between the known and unknown,
awakening the flame within.

God's mystery beckons
in the morning mist.
Life's jewels abound!
Light and object have become one.

A union of beauty
between naive and innocence,
between heaven and earth,
between dreams and reality,
between known and unknown,
between macabre and devotion,
between icon and idol.

Claim your oneness,
your connectedness.

Value love in every form of life
as an expression of the One
whose life and love
is beyond all form.

Look closely.
Between the known and the unknown.

The morning prisms hang like slivers of broken glass,
reflecting the hope of a morning song,
the notes hang like tears,
chanting words of others fears.

Somewhere in the between,
one drop takes leave of the others,
sliding down to the edge, letting go.
Falling into its true self.
Suspended.

Acceptance and surrender
are portals for the
unconditional love of God to enter.

All that is beautiful and radiant
has a pre-ordained place in His world
which belongs first and foremost,
to the poor and humbled.

Only in this knowing
can you cross over
in the between.

foundation

As caring beings,
we are continuously torn between what is and what could be.
The truth is usually found somewhere "in the between".
As humans we are very complex,
always questioning our future,
our faith,
our decisions,
our well being,
our very existence.

We're "in between" life and death,
"in between" the depth of desperation and the exhaltation of joy,
"in between" sadness and happiness.

Our foundation is honored to be the publisher of
In the Between, a labor of love celebrating the human frailty that
inspires us to reflect, to listen, to experience,
to participate, but also because it celebrates the beauty
of God's work and the goodness in people.

People that have and will always selflessly donate
their talent, time, and money for the benefit of those
less fortunate.

John & Geri Cusenza Foundation
Celebrating *In the Between*

The Sisters of Notre Dame

The Sisters of Notre Dame were founded in 1850 in Germany. Today, our members are ministering all over the world. And though we each may walk on different roads, we share a common path, and, in imitation of Our Lady, follow the Christ.

Our Sisters have ministered in California since 1924. Our ministries have focused on the spiritual, educational, and humanitarian needs of those we serve.

We have joyfully taught the young, nursed the sick, and assisted the poor. And through our pastoral and social work, we have touched the souls of those who have seemed to have been forgotten by all but Him.

And so, by doing His work, we have made our greatest dream come true: to share with others our deep experience of God's goodness and provident care.

acknowledgements

It was the vision and goal of Geri and John Sebastian Cusenza to finance the needs of the poor women and children in Arusha, Tanzania, East Africa and ensure their future through the creation and marketing of *In the Between*. They have invested fully not just of the financial resources to create and publish it, but selfless love, time, energy, and creativity. They nursed the text through many drafts, urged me to perfect the photography, challenging with clarity and a critical eye every step of the way. That the book is what it is is a tribute to Geri's great patience and amazing art direction. I also offer grateful thanks to the following:

Dachelle Duffy, our designer, for her unending insights and inspirational visions.

Anthony Guthmiller for his valuable inspiration and expertise.

Fran and Jack Morehart for the quiet of their home as a writing retreat.

John W. Tulac and Lionel S. Sobel for their legal counsel.

Therese Errigo, Jon Kirwan, Kevin Sherman, Edward and Sally McSweeney, Cecelia and Dieter Huckestein, Barbara Margolies, Joseph Sokoine, Esther and Alfred Leo, Joe Kennedy, Jerry Stadler, Dave West, Steven Muro Gabe Lakatosh, Joe Valdez, Debbie Jagoras, Peter John Tortorella, Jr., Michael Vezo, Jane Ferrone, Jan Nathan, Roy and Bobbie Guzman, Father Maurice Chase, Janet Buc, Tom Franey, Claire Sutherland, Cathy Davis, who helped and gave support or services along the way.

Richard Ferry, Korn Ferry International, Los Angeles

Peter Mullin, Mullin Consulting, Los Angeles

Bernard P. Vanderfin, for his gracious access to his award winning orchid collection at Gallup & Stribling Orchids

William A. Grimm, Laura Turitz, Captured Images, Inc.

Mark Holden, Karen Story, Holden Color

Samy Kamienowicz, Louis Feldman, Samy's Camera

Victor Borod, Nikon, Inc.

Jim Hanon, William McKendry, Jason Vanderground, Jacqui Garcia, Bill Oechsler and staff at Hanon McKendry and Straightline.

Tania Presby, Dennis Farrier, Bruce Gordon, Rebecca Mendez, Adams Eeuwens, Mark Durkin, Randy Ginsberg, for their unending inspiration and encouragement.

John Fosmire, President of Anderson Lithograph, Diane Gavia, Phil Martinez and Walter Gustafson, and the color, prepress, and press departments of Anderson Lithograph in Los Angeles.

Sister Mary Sujita Kallupurakkathu, Sister Mary Francis Murray, Sister Mary Kristin Battles, Sister Mary La Reina Kelly, Sister Mary Joan Schlotfeldt, who gave special support and encouragement.

Sister Mary Shobana, Sister Mary Rashmi, Sister Mary Kusum, Sister Mary Shaija, Sister Mary Neelima, Sister Mary Sawmya and our Notre Dame Candidates in Arusha, Tanzania who have the care and welfare of the women and children so much at heart. The sisters made me feel genuinely welcome and graciously provided the opportunities for me to photograph the beautiful people and flowers of East Africa, some of which are included in this book.

In the Between

Sisters of Notre Dame
1776 Hendrix Avenue, Thousand Oaks, CA 91360

PHOTOGRAPHY & TEXT
Sister Rose Marie Tulacz, S.N.D.

ART DIRECTOR
Geri Cusenza

DESIGN
Dachelle Duffy Design

WRITER/EDITOR
Anthony Guthmiller

BIOGRAPHY
Michael S. Emerson

LOCATION
Villa Dei Fiori

COLOR, PREPRESS & PRINTING
Anderson Lithograph, Los Angeles

Original photographs in this book may be purchased.
For information please write:

Sister Rose Marie Tulacz, S.N.D.
1776 Hendrix Avenue, Thousand Oaks, CA 91360
ndcreation@aol.com

Library of Congress Control Number: 2002090799
ISBN 0-9719020-0-3
10 9 8 7 6 5 4 3 2 1

First Printing

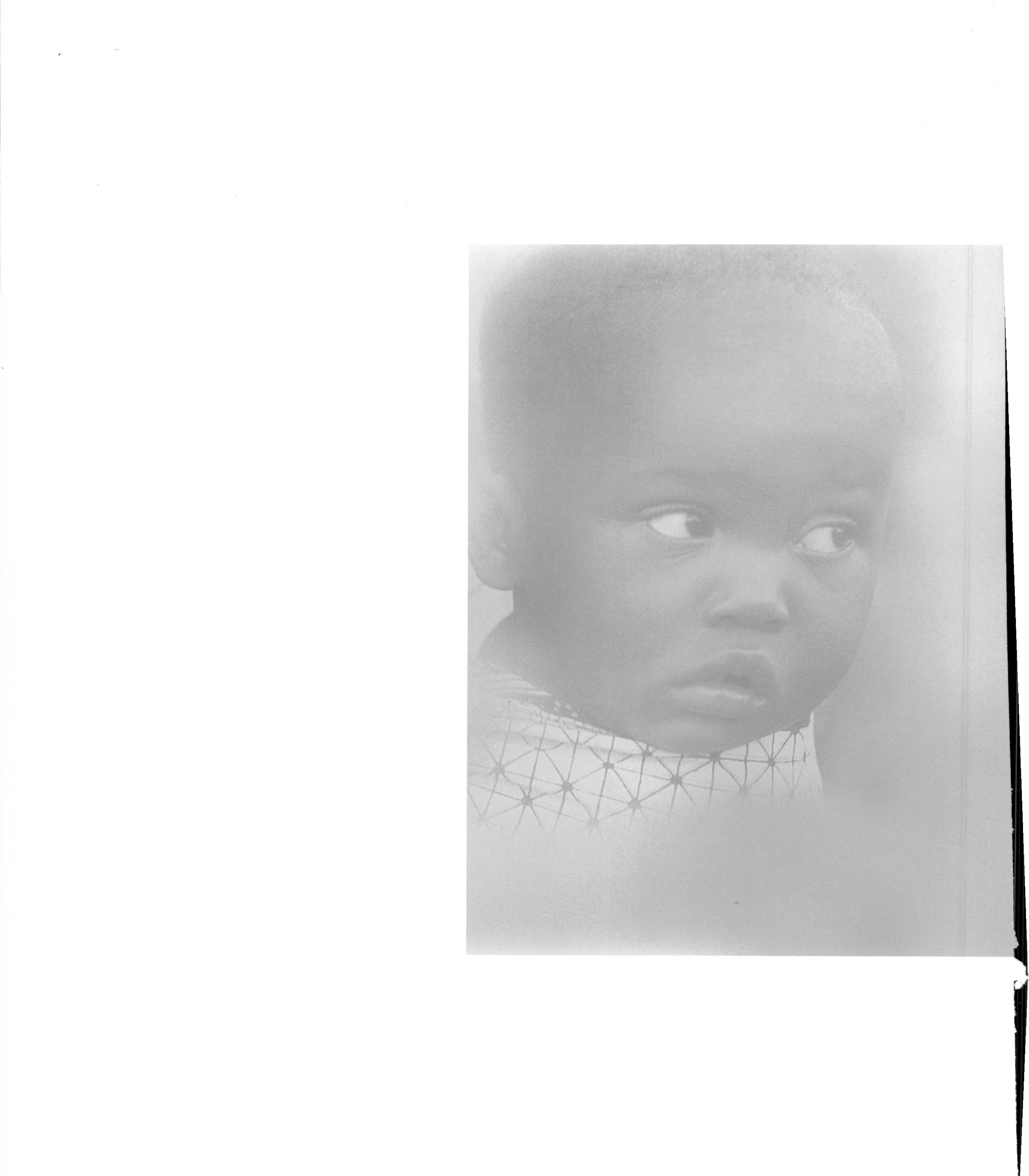